Into The Garden

Into The Garden

Timeless Reflections and Lore

Nicola Gillies

Robinson

FOR ELIZABETH, HELEN AND RICHARD

Robinson Publishing
7, Kensington Church Court, London W8 4SP

Produced in association with Saraband Inc.

ISBN 1-85487-992-8

Printed in China

9 8 7 6 5 4 3 2 1

The publisher would like to thank Robin Langley Sommer and Peter C. Gillies for their suggestions and contributions to this volume.

CONTENTS

Garden Delights

Gardens of Eden

Our England is a garden that is full of stately views.
Of border beds and shrubberies and lawns and avenues,
With statues on the terraces and peacocks strutting by;
But the Glory of the Garden lies in more than meets the eye.

Our England is a garden, and such gardens are not made
By singing:—"Oh, how beautiful!" and sitting in the shade,
While better men than we go out and start their working lives
At grubbing weeds from gravel-paths with broken dinner-knives.

Rudyard Kipling,
"The Glory of the Garden"

Its natural features are not striking; but Art has effected such wonderful things that the uninstructed visitor would never guess that nearly the whole scene was but the embodied thought of a human mind. A skilful painter hardly does more for his blank sheet of canvas, than the landscape-gardener, the planter, the arranger of trees, has done for the monotonous surface of Blenheim; making the most of every undulation; flinging down a hillock, a big lump of earth out of a giant's hand, wherever it was needed; putting in beauty as often as there was a niche for it; opening vistas to every point that deserved to be seen, and throwing a veil of impenetrable foliage around what ought to be hidden;—and then, to be sure, the lapse of a century has softened the harsh outline of man's labors, and has given the place back to Nature again with the addition of what consummate science could achieve.... Positively, the garden of Eden cannot have been more beautiful than this private garden of Blenheim.

Nathaniel Hawthorne on Blenheim Park,
Our Old Home

Hail Kew! thou darling of the tuneful nine,
Thou eating-house of verse, where poets dine;
The groves of Kew, however misapplied,
To serve the purposes of lust and pride,
Were, by the greater monarch's care, designed
A place of conversation for the mind;
Where solitude and silence should remain,
And conscience keep her sessions and arraign.

THOMAS CHATTERTON, "Kew Gardens"

I know a little garden close
Set thick with lily and red rose,
Where I would wander if I might
From dewy dawn to dewy night,
And have one with me wandering.

WILLIAM MORRIS,
"The Life and Death of Jason"

Just now the lilac is in bloom,
All before my little room;
And in my flower beds, I think,
Smile the carnation and the pink;
And down the borders, well I know
The poppy and the pansy blow…

❧ Rupert Brooke,
"The Old Vicarage, Grantchester"

Floral Delights

Rue and roses; is it so,
Where roses blossom, must rue grow,
And shade the roses, as they blow?

So long as love and sorrow meet,
So long must rue and roses sweet
Together bloom to be complete.

Caroline Hazard, "Rue and Roses"

…Each beauteous flow'r,
Iris all hues, Roses, and Jessamin
Rear'd high their flourished heads between, and wrought
Mosaic; underfoot the Violet,
Crocus, and Hyacinth with rich inlay
Broider'd the ground, more color'd than with stone
Of costliest Emblem…

John Milton

Rose,
Unbent by winds, unchill'd by snows,
Far from the winters of the west,
By every breeze and season blest,
Return the sweets by nature given
In softest incense back to Heaven…

GEORGE GORDON, LORD BYRON

I have a garden of my own,
but so with roses overgrown,
and lilies, that you would it guess
to be a little wilderness.

ANDREW MARVELL

I never wanted to be a bug
Until I found one safe and snug
In the velvet heart of a pale pink rose
With petals tucked about his toes.

❧ Marion Lee

In late October, when the frosts have blighted the dahlias, it is a delight to come upon the delicate grayish-purple blossoms, so like the first crocuses of spring, in the otherwise devastated garden.

❧ Helen Morgenthau Fox on Saffron Crocus

Yet mark'd I where the bolt of Cupid fell:
It fell upon a little western flower—
Before, milk-white, now purple with love's wound—
And maidens call it love-in-idleness.
Fetch me that flower; the herb I show'd thee once:
The juice of it on sleeping eyelids laid
Will make a man or woman madly dote
Upon the next live creature that it sees.

Shakespeare on pansies,
A Midsummer's Night's Dream

Elizabethan lady
In farthingale of leaves,
Stiff ruffs and cuffs of blossom
And downy velvet sleeves,
Let horehound sit for moonlight
To songs no longer sung.
I almost taste its flavor
Half-bitter on my tongue.

Elisabeth W. Morse, "Horehound"

Mother Nature's Garden

I cannot see what flowers are at my feet
Nor what soft incense hangs upon the boughs,
But, in embalmed darkness, guess each sweet
Wherewith the seasonable month endows
The grass, the thicket, and the fruit-tree wild
White hawthorn, and the pastoral eglantine:
Fast fading violets covered up in leaves;
And mid-May's eldest child,
The coming musk-rose, full of dewy wine,
The murmurous haunt of flies on summer eves.

JOHN KEATS,
"Ode to a Nightingale"

Before my door the box-edg'd border lies,
Where flowers of mint and thyme and tansy rise;
Along my wall the yellow stonecrop grows,
And the red houseleek on my brown thatch blows.

Among green osiers winds my stream away,
Where the blue halcyon skims from spray to spray,
Where waves the bulrush as the waters glide,
And yellow flag-flow'rs deck the sunny side.

JOHN SCOTT

I wander'd lonely as a cloud
That floats on high o'er vales and hills,
When all at once I saw a crowd,
A host, of golden daffodils;
Beside the lake, beneath the trees,
Fluttering and dancing in the breeze.

WILLIAM WORDSWORTH

Winged Envoys

I managed to keep a few square yards on a shelf for staging in an unheated greenhouse, and those few square yards were crowded with tiny bright things from New Year's Day to Easter. Their brilliance contrasted with the snow and the leaden skies; it was like coming into an aviary of tropical birds or butterflies...

VITA SACKVILLE-WEST

Now I am in the garden at the back...a very preserve of butterflies, as I remember it, with a high fence, and a gate and padlock; where the fruit clusters on the trees, riper and richer than fruit has ever been since, in any other garden, and where my mother gathers some in a basket, while I stand by, bolting furtive gooseberries, and trying to look unmoved.

CHARLES DICKENS

The robin flew down from his tree-top and hopped about or flew after her from one bush to another. He chirped a good deal and had a very busy air, as if he were showing her things.... He was very much pleased to see gardening begun on his own estate. He had often wondered at Ben Weatherstaff. Where gardening is done all sorts of delightful things to eat are turned up with the soil. Now here was this new kind of creature who was not half Ben's size and yet had the sense to come into his garden and begin at once.

❧ Frances Hodgson Burnett, *The Secret Garden*

The mute bird sitting on the stone,
The dank moss dripping from the wall,
The garden-walk with weeds o'ergrown,
I love them How I love them all!

❧ Emily Brontë, *Poems*, 1846

Garden Wildlife

The world has different owners at sunrise.... Even your own garden does not belong to you. Rabbits and blackbirds have the lawns; a tortoise-shell cat who never appears in daytime patrols the brick walls, and a golden-tailed pheasant glints his way through the iris spears.

ANNE MORROW LINDBERGH

If you would keep your soul
From spotted sight or sound,
Live like the velvet mole;
Go burrow underground.

from ELINOR WYLIE, "The Eagle and the Mole"

Just above this open space is a low hedgerow of Hazels, with still rising wooded ground above. What a pretty and pleasant place that wise rabbit has chosen for his "bury," as country folk call it; at the foot of the low sandy bank, and where it is kept quite dry by the roots of the old Hazels.

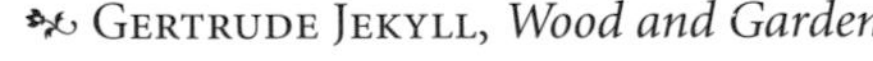

GERTRUDE JEKYLL, *Wood and Garden*

The honey-bee's great ambition is to be rich, to lay up great stores, to possess the sweet of every flower that blooms. She is more than provident. Enough will not satisfy her; she must have all she can get by hook or by crook.

JOHN BURROUGHS

A very little thing, a little worm,
Or hourglass-blazoned spider, it is said,
Can kill a tiger.

ROBERT LOWELL

A bird does not sing because it has an answer—it sings because it has a song.

ANCIENT CHINESE PROVERB

And a mouse is miracle enough to stagger sextillions of infidels.

WALT WHITMAN

Walled Gardens

The very rich not merely had their roof-gardens, their inner garden of the peristyle, but in some parts of the City they had grounds round their houses which a few of the immensely rich enlarged to become small parks. The models were those Eastern 'gardens of paradise' which so enchanted the Greeks and Romans. They offered a delightful spectacle of grass, trees of all kinds both ornamental and fruit-bearing, vines, ivy and other creeping plants, flowers, a fountain, some statuary or a shrine and some animals and birds, particularly doves, pheasants, ducks, partridges and the gorgeously coloured birds of the East, of which the peacock was the most renowned. Some would be wild, others in cages or aviaries. The whole was designed and laid out formally to provide at once a pleasure to the eyes, pleasant scents and a pleasant murmur of water, bees and birds, except for the harsh noise of the peacocks.

F.R. Cowell,
Everyday Life in Ancient Rome

She thought she saw something sticking out of the black earth—some sharp little pale green points. She remembered what Ben Weatherstaff had said, and she knelt down to look at them.

"Yes, they are tiny growing things and they might be crocuses or snowdrops or daffodils," she whispered.

She bent very close to them and sniffed the fresh scent of the damp earth. She liked it very much.

FRANCIS HODGSON BURNETT,
The Secret Garden

The little low and creeping thymes now comfortably
sprawl
Upon the crevices stepping stones beyond the
sheltering wall,
Sun-warmed, mist-laved, brushed by the southwest
breeze.

GLADYS JENKINS, "The Little Creeping Thymes"

Garden Wisdom

Nutrients and Nurture

Doves dung is ye best, the same possesseth a mighty hoteness. The dung also of hen and other foules greatly commended for the sournesse, excepts ye dung of geese, ducks and other water foules. A commendation next is attributed to the Asses dung, in that the same beast for his leisurely eating, digesteth easier, and causeth the better dung. The third place is the goates dung, after this both ye Oxe and Cow dung; next the Swines dung, worthier than the Oxen or Kine. The vilest and worst of all dungs after the opinion of the Greek writers of Husbandry, is the Horse and Moiles.

The dung which men make (if the same be not mixed with the Rabbith, or dust swept out of the house) is greatly mislyked, for that by nature, it is hoter, and burneth the seedes sowne in that earth: so that this is not to be used, unlesse the grounde be barren, gravelly or verie lose sand, lacking strength in it. The mud also of running water, as the ditch or river, may bee employed instead of dung.

THOMAS HILL, *The Gardener's Labyrinth*

Different flowers respond to different nutrients. Placing wood ash on lily beds helps them to flourish. For hardy fuchsia plants, try placing bracken leaves around their roots. To increase the vigour and fragrance of roses, camellias, rhododendrons and azaleas, try emptying cold tea and tea leaves around the roots. There is an old belief that if chamomile is dispersed about the garden it will keep plants healthy.

Helen Morgenthau Fox

Old-time gardeners found that burying their worn-out leather boots increased the productivity of their soil. As the leather decomposes, the many nutrients in the material will nourish the soil.

Bacteria-free compost can be achieved by soaking it in boiling water to sterilise, and leaving it to cool. Drain off the excess water and place the compost in shallow boxes to dry.

Feeding cabbages a regular dose of beer is believed to encourage their growth. Try this unusual plant food on all your vegetables and flowers.

Astrological Sowing Times

Aries*—March 21 to April 20*

A cardinal fire sign. Seeds sown during this sign, including grapes, produce good stalks and vines.

Taurus*—April 21 to May 21*

A fixed earth sign. The best time to sow root-crop seed.

Gemini*—May 22 to June 21*

A barren sign. A good time to sow melon seed.

Cancer*—June 22 to July 22*

A cardinal water sign. The most productive time for any sort of sowing or transplanting.

Leo*—July 23 to August 23*

A barren sign. Not a good time for any sort of sowing.

Virgo*—August 24 to September 23*

A barren sign. Not a productive time to sow, but good for flower blossom.

Libra*—September 24 to October 23*

A cardinal air sign. The ideal time to sow flower seed, but a bad time for fruit.

Scorpio*—October 24 to November 22*

A fixed water sign. The second-best sowing time, especially for pumpkins and other gourdlike plants.

Saggitarius*—November 23 to December 21*

A masculine fire sign. An unfavourable time to sow or plant anything.

Capricorn*—December 22 to January 20*

A cardinal earth sign. A good time to plant and sow plants that produce an abundance of roots and branches.

Aquarius*—January 21 to February 19*

A masculine air sign. Unfavourable generally for seed, though a good time for laying out onions.

Pisces*—February 20 to March 20*

A cardinal water sign. Beneficial time for sowing, as plants that grow from seeds sown at this time are best adapted to withstand drought.

Gardening by the Moon

It is best to turn and work the soil when the moon is in the barren signs of Leo, Virgo, Aquarius or Gemini.

For the healthiest plants, always sow seed with a waxing moon, never when it's waning.

The Egyptian and Greek instructions of Husbandry report, that the seeds after the bestowing, will remain ungnawn or bitter and free of harm by creeping things in the garden, if the seeds shall be committed to the earth when the Moon possesseth her half light, or it is a quarter old.

THOMAS HILL, *The Gardener's Labyrinth*

When the ring round the moon is far—rain is soon,
When the ring round the moon is near—rain is far away.

TRADITIONAL

Water Wise

To have water, whether of pond or stream, in a garden is the greatest possible gain, for it enables the ingenious garden owner or designer not only to grow in perfection many beautiful plants, but to treat the watery places, according to their nature and capability, in various delightful ways. The kind of stream that is easiest to deal with is one which has a shallow flow over a stony bottom and that is not much below the general ground-level. Here we have, ready-made, the most desirable conditions, and it is an easy matter to plant the banks and water edges without any work of shifting or shaping ground.

GERTRUDE JEKYLL, *A Gardener's Testament*

I come into the presence of still water. And I feel
above me the day-blind stars waiting with their light.
For a time, I rest in the grace of the world, and am free.

WENDELL BERRY

There are any number of things that may be recommended for planting along the banks of running water. Some belong to our native flora, but are so distinctly desirable, that if they do not occur naturally in the place, they should be searched for. These are the yellow Flag (*Iris Pseudacorus*) with showy flowers in June and upright sword-like leaves; the Water Plantain (*Alisma Plantago*) with large ribbed leaves, something like those of Veratrum, and a wide-spreading, lace-like panicle of flower; then the beautiful rosy pink Flowering Rush (*Butomus*), looking like something tropical. For a grand plant of stately habit there is a Great Water Dock (*Rumex Hydrolapathum*), with very large leaves that, as the season advances, take on brilliant colourings of yellow and red.

GERTRUDE JEKYLL,
A Gardener's Testament

Seasonal Observations

The blooms of sweet peas will be the biggest and most fragrant when planted on St. Patrick's Day (March 17).

Onion skins very thin,
Mild winter coming in.
Onion skins very tough,
Coming winter very rough.

Cut thistles in May, they grow in a day;
Cut them in June, that is too soon;
Cut them in July, then they die.

After a frosty winter there will be a good fruit harvest.

Mist in March, frost in May.

It is a wet month to be when there are two full moons in it.

Timeless Lore

Varro, an ancient Roman agriculturalist, found that "large walnut trees close by make the border of the farm sterile."

The ancient Romans soaked their plant bulbs in wine to produce purple flowers.

Talking to plants helps them flourish.

When your fingers nettles find,
Be sure a dock is close behind.

Traditional rhyme on *Rumex*

When snails climb up the stalks of grass,
wet weather is at hand.

Some believe that having a pregnant woman hug the trunk of a tree will increase the growth and vitality of that tree.

Invited Guests

The surest way to attract butterflies to visit your garden is to plant Buddleia (one of whose common names is Butterfly Bush), because the profuse flowers are sweetly scented and brightly coloured. Other flowers, including asters, chrysanthemums and violas, also draw these delicate winged creatures.

If you enjoy having birds in your garden but wish to deter them from scavenging seeds and soft fruits, try incorporating a bird feeder and bird bath. Not only will the birds find life-sustaining nourishment during the lean months, but their presence will enliven and diversify the garden environment. Remember that a variety of seeds in the feeder will attract different species. Precautions should be taken to minimise the exposure to cats, and to make the feeder squirrel-proof.

Worms are the best ally a gardener has in ensuring healthy plant growth, because their movement breaks up—and thus aerates—the soil, providing a greater supply of oxygen and other valuable nutrients to the roots. Worms can be purchased and added to the soil with compost.

Uninvited Guests

To prevent mice and birds from eating your seeds, moisten them with kerosene before sowing.

Slugs are easily distracted by beer. Place capfuls on the ground to lure slugs away from plants. As an added precaution, a perimeter of sand around vegetable gardens will keep slugs from entering.

MARY ASPESI

Planting a border of marigolds around your garden will help deter such pests—both above and underground—as the blackfly and wireworm. The once-popular practice of using mothballs for this purpose poses a hazard to animal life.

To keep birds away from crocus plants, try planting lavender nearby.

If your vegetable garden is suffering from rabbits, try incorporating plants that repel them. Foxgloves (*Digitalis*) or onions are two plants that will ensure a rabbit-free area. If you enjoy watching the hopping creatures in your garden, but want to keep them away from your plants, you could try planting a liberal amount of dill (*Anethum graveolens*) in your garden. Rabbits love the taste of this plant and will head straight for it, leaving all thoughts of your vegetables and flowers behind.

To keep deer from nibbling on your plants, place soap shavings along the perimeter of your garden.

Fragrances

In order to make unscented flowers fragrant, soak the seeds overnight in scented water, for example rose water, and then let them dry in the sun. When grown, the flowers will emit the scent of the solution.

To improve the vitality and fragrance of roses, try one or all of these tricks: place banana skins just below the surface of the surrounding soil; add lard or meat fat to the soil; or place parsley around the stalk to improve the fragrance.

Used at weddings, Rosemary was either gilded or dipped in scented water and carried in the Bride's wreath. It silently bade the bride bear away to her new home the remembrance of the dear old roof tree which had sheltered her youth and the loving hearts which had cherished her.

HELEN NOYES WEBSTER

Indoor Pleasures from the Garden

To make a potpourri, peel and dry the fresh root of Iris and store for two years. After grinding, the powdered root emits a violet fragrance. Rose petals and spices blend with this aroma while orris root is a good fixative for potpourri.

AN 18TH-CENTURY RECIPE

To make a Lavender Sack: Take a basket of lavender flowers, not full blown. Strip the flowers from the stalks. Dry them in the air but not in the sun. Add some of the dried leaves of the plant. Pack them all in a little sack of fine silk or muslin, very closely stuffed. You may put them under your pillows for sleep, and with your linens for perfume.

PRISCILLA SAWYER LORD

It seemed a shame to mar the perfect symmetry of this stately plant [Angelica] by cutting its stalks, but I was eager to try my hand at making from them some of the sweetmeats that were popular centuries ago. Very carefully I cut four long hollow stalks and took them to the kitchen to be candied....I decorated a cake with them in the English fashion.

ANNIE BURNHAM CARTER

To Pickle Nasturtiums: Gather the berries when full grown but young, put them in a pot, pour boiling salt and water on, and let them stand three or four days; then drain off the water, and cover them with cold vinegar; add a few blades of mace, and whole grains of black pepper.

MRS. MARY RANDOLPH

To dry flowers for your dried arrangements, hang them upside down in a cool, dry place. This will prevent the flower from bending, ensuring a straight and pleasing effect.

Seed Skills

Seed grows best in warm soil. An age-old way to test the temperature of your soil is to place your elbow in it.

Most newly sown seeds will germinate more readily if they are watered immediately after sowing with warm water from a fine rose sprinkler. After this initial watering, tepid water must be applied, never cold water.

For the seeds of thirstier plants, line the soil with sheets of moisture-retaining newspaper.

The quality of larger seeds can be tested by placing them in a dish of water. Good seeds will sink, while less desirable ones will float to the surface.

As well as taking measures to distract birds from your garden, sow seed generously: the ancient law of tithing was to set aside ten percent of the crop for the birds.

Good Neighbours

Bruising cloves of garlic before planting them and placing olive stones around each plant will increase the size of the plants and enhance their flavor.

Planting Marigold among your vegetables will help to keep slugs away.

The strawberry grows underneath the nettle;
And wholesome berries thrive and ripen best
Neighbour'd by fruit of baser quality.

SHAKESPEARE, *King Henry V*

Tomatoes, Basil, Nettles

Tomato plants will thrive when planted with herbs such as basil, and the root secretions from nettle plants will encourage the tomato plant to produce more flavourful fruit, while increasing resistance to mould.

Apples, Chives, Nasturtiums

Nasturtiums repel aphids, a common apple tree pest, while chives will help the trunk of an apple tree that is suffering from apple scab.

Carrots, Onion, Leeks

Onion plants will repel the carrot fly maggot from carrot plants, while leeks will keep the onion fly and leek moth away.

Potatoes, Peas

The roots of pea plants secrete nitrogen into the soil, a nutrient that potato plants thrive upon.

Strawberries, Lavender, Pyrethrum

Lavender will keep birds away from strawberry plants, while pyrethrum effectively repels aphids.

Garlic, Roses, Peaches

Garlic's root secretions help repel aphids and onion flies from rose bushes and protect against root curl on peach trees.

Sunflowers, Sweet Peas

Planting sweet peas near sunflowers will protect the delicate sweet pea from wind damage and attract pest-controlling birds.

Unhappy Bedfellows

Beetroot, Beans

Beetroot will not thrive when planted with beans, as the taller bean plants cast too much shade on the smaller beetroot plants.

Apples, Carrots, Potatoes

The flavour of stored carrots will become bitter from the ethylene gas that picked apples release. Also, potatoes planted near apples will be more likely to suffer from *Phytophthora*, the same fungus that caused the famine in Ireland.

Clover, Buttercups, Camellias

The roots of buttercups secrete a substance that inhibits the growth of nitrogen bacteria, and it will starve clover plants if placed in the same area. Never allow clover to grow up camellias, as the mites on clover plants cause camellia plants to bud prematurely.

Hyssop, Cabbages, Radishes

Planting hyssop near cabbages will attract the cabbage white butterfly, while the growth of radishes will be stunted when planted near hyssop.

Onions, Peas, Beans

Planting onion plants near peas and beans will inhibit the growth of both vegetables.

Raspberries, Blackcurrants, Potatoes

Raspberries and blackcurrants should not be planted near each other as they will compete for space and nutrients. Potato plants will become more vulnerable to potato blight if planted near raspberries.

Shallots, Peas

Never place shallots and peas in the garden together, as each inhibits the other's growth.

Strawberries, Gladioli

Never grow gladioli and strawberry in the same garden. Even if they are planted at a distance from each other, the gladioli will cause the strawberries to die.

Tomatoes, Fennel, Potatoes

The growth of tomato vines will be stunted if they are planted near fennel. Also, tomato plants increase the potatoes' susceptibility to potato blight.

Storing Up for Winter

After harvesting seeds for the next season, it is best to store them in paper bags in a dry and cool area. Suspending the bags from the ceiling will keep most pests away. The longevity of seeds depends on the type of plant. Most vegetable seeds can be kept for up to two years, but cucumber and melon seed will last for ten or more years without losing their capacity to germinate.

Store onions as you would apples and potatoes, placing them in shallow boxes or string bags. Like garlic, onions can also be worked into a "rope" and stored hanging. Beetroot is best stored upright in deep boxes of either sand, ashes, or sifted soil. As a general rule, always make sure that your storage area is dry, dark and cool, and keep the individual fruits and vegetables separate from each other. Excessive light, moisture and heat will dramatically shorten their shelf-life.

Dual Roles

Achillea millefolium (yarrow) combines the advantages of flower and herb. Since ancient times, it has been esteemed as a dressing for wounds: according to legend, Achilles used it to staunch bleeding in his wounded soldiers. It was often fed to livestock to improve their health and was taken to alleviate fever and toothache. It is a good companion to most other herbs, in which it increases aroma and oil content. A solution made from yarrow leaves is useful for soils that are deficient in copper, and the plant attracts beneficial insects like ladybirds.

Many easily cultivated flowers are as delightful in a culinary context—especially in salads and as decorative garnish—as they are aesthetically pleasing in a flower border. Flower canapés make delicious and attractive treats. To prepare these, roll out and cut pastry into small circles or star shapes and bake in a moderately hot oven until lightly browned. When sufficiently cooled, place a small slice or wedge of cheese or paté on each pastry case and arrange on a serving platter. Add a viola or nasturtium, rose or marigold petals to each canapé immediately before serving.

The Language of Flowers and Plants

Flowers and plants provide a pleasing array of colour and texture in your garden and, therefore, a beautiful environment. The symbolic meaning of flowers and plants may, however, be just as important in determining what you choose to plant. What the garden says about the gardener can be quite revealing.

The rose is a favorite choice for flower gardens. Its fragrant, beautiful bloom signifies love, secrecy and life. White roses stand for innocence, red for romantic love, yellow for friendship and golden for perfection.

Sunflowers are, of course, identified with the sun, because of their bright solar hue and their shape, which resembles the sun and its rays. This boldly colourful flower symbolises happiness, vitality and light.

Mistletoe's association with fertility and freedom derives from its sacred significance to the ancient Celts and Druids. The Christmas tradition of kissing under the mistletoe may have originated with the Roman festival of Saturnalia.

The clinging and climbing characteristics of ivy represent friendship and constancy, while its prolific growth symbolises fertility and life.

Flowering Features

Sweet woodruff is an ideal ground cover for shady places. It is a gem of a plant in every respect, with neat whorls of lanceolate leaves and sheets of minute white star-shaped blossoms in spring. Sweet woodruff is one of the herbs valued by flower arrangers who enjoy using distinctive foliage. A cutting or two... in an arrangement is reputed to help keep the water fresh.

PRISCILLA SAWYER LORD

To prolong the life of cut flowers, try adding a pinch of salt to their water. Adding aspirin to the water of limp plants will often revive them.

Never place daffodils in arrangements with other flowers, as their stems excrete poisons that will kill the others.

A handful of rusty nails placed in the soil around the roots of your pink or white hydrangeas will turn the color of their blossoms to blue.

Garden Reflections

Homage

"Why, one can hear and see the grass growing!" thought Levin, noticing a wet, slate-colored aspen leaf moving beside a blade of young grass.

LEO TOLSTOY, *Anna Karenina*

Seasons and Times

Deep in the greens of summer sing the
lives I've come to love.

THEODORE ROETHKE, American poet

In the evening calm, hardly a breath of air touched the garden. The heat was intense, and the quiet gave the light and dark greens of the foliage a special limpidity. The green of the lawn seemed to rise up and flow through her.

JUNICHIRO TANIZAKI

Oh, to be in England
Now that April's there,
And whoever wakes in England
Sees, some morning, unaware,
That the lowest boughs and the brush-wood sheaf
Round the elm-tree bole are in tiny leaf,
While the chaffinch sings on the orchard bough
In England—now!

ROBERT BROWNING,
"Home-Thoughts, from Abroad"

Epigraphs

I began to reflect on Nature's eagerness to sow life everywhere, to fill the planet with it, to crowd with it the earth, the air, and the seas. Into every empty corner, into all forgotten things and nooks, Nature struggles to pour life, pouring life into the dead, life into life itself. That immense, overwhelming, relentless, burning ardency of Nature for the stir of life!

HENRY BESTON

I do not know whether I was then a man dreaming I was a butterfly, or whether I am now a butterfly dreaming I am a man.

❧ Chuang Tzu, Chinese sage

The pedigree of honey
Does not concern the bee;
A clover, any time, to him
Is aristocracy.

❧ Emily Dickinson

Who loves a garden still his Eden keeps,
Perennial pleasures plants, and wholesome harvest reaps.

❧ Bronson Alcott

Summer set lip to earth's bosom bare,
And left the flushed print in a poppy there.

❧ Francis Thompson, "The Poppy"

In the name of the bee,
And of the butterfly,
And of the breeze,
Amen.

EMILY DICKINSON, "Envoi"

The fine old place never looked more like a delightful home than at that moment: the great white lilies were in flower; the nasturtiums, their pretty leaves all silvered with dew, were running away over the low stone wall; the very noises all around had a heart of peace within them.

GEORGE ELIOT

Weeds

What is a weed? A plant whose virtues have not yet been discovered.

RALPH WALDO EMERSON

It takes me longer to weed than most people, because I will do it so thoroughly. It is such a pleasure and satisfaction to clear the beautiful brown earth, smooth and soft, from these rough growths, leaving the beautiful green Poppies and Larkspurs and Pinks and Asters, and the rest, in undisturbed possession!

CELIA THAXTER

[Mignonette was]...known as the fragrant weed when introduced into England in 1751. It came to the British Isles through Holland though it is a native of Egypt. It became a favorite for balcony and window boxes. Planted in this manner it developed long trailing habits and perfumed the air about it. The smallest variety is the sweetest and the fragrance is better in a moist bed.

ADELMA G. SIMMONS

Philosophy

Alas, how seldom do these little schemes come off. Something will go wrong; some puppy will bury a bone; some mouse will eat the bulbs; some mole will heave the daphnes and the lilac out of the ground.

Still, no gardener would be a gardener if he did not live in hope.

Vita Sackville-West

I came to love my rows, my beans, though so many more than I wanted. They attached me to the earth, and so I got strength like Antaeus.

Henry David Thoreau

The main purpose of a garden is to give its owner the best and highest kind of earthly pleasure.

It is not enough to cultivate plants well; they must also be used well. It is just the careful and thoughtful exercise of the higher qualities that makes a garden interesting, and their absence that leaves it blank, and dull, and lifeless. I am heartily in sympathy with the feeling described in these words in a friend's letter, "I think there are few things so interesting as to see in what way a person, whose perceptions you think fine and worthy of study, will give them expression in a garden."

The size of a garden has very little to do with its merit. It is merely an accident relating to the circumstances of the owner. It is the size of his heart and brain and goodwill that will make his garden either delightful or dull, as the case may be, and either leave it at the usual monotonous dead-level, or raise it, in whatever degree may be, towards that of a work of fine art. If a man knows much, it is more difficult for him to deal with a small space than a larger, for he will have to make the more sacrifice; but if he is wise he will at once make up his mind about what he will let go, and how he may best treat the restricted space.

GERTRUDE JEKYLL

The Circle of Nature

There is not a single colour hidden away in the chalice of a flower…to which, by some subtle sympathy with the very soul of things, my nature does not answer.

❧ Oscar Wilde

This is my letter to the world,
That never wrote to me,—
The simple news that Nature told,
With tender majesty.

❧ Emily Dickinson

Deep in their roots,
All flowers keep the light.

❧ Theodore Roethke

Birth, life, and death — each took place on the hidden side of a leaf.

❧ Toni Morrison

All gardening involves constant change. It is even more so in woodland. A young bit of wood such as mine is for ever changing. Happily, each new development reveals new beauty of aspect or new possibility of good treatment, such as, rightly apprehended and then guided, tends to a better state than before.

❧ Gertrude Jekyll

A seed hidden in the heart of an apple is an orchard invisible.

❧ Welsh proverb

Herbal Treasure

I plant Rosemary all over my garden, so pleasant is it to know that at every few steps one may draw the kindly branchlets through one's hand, and have the enjoyment of their incomparable incense; and I grow it against walls, so that the sun may draw out its inexhaustible sweetness to greet me as I pass.

GERTRUDE JEKYLL

As for Rosemarine, I lett it runne all over my garden wals, not onlie because my bees love it, but because it is the herb sacred to remembrance and, therefore, to friendship.

SIR THOMAS MORE

In short, it is a Plant indeed with so many wonderful Properties, that the assiduous use of it is said to render Men Immortal.

JOHN EVELYN, on sage

Even you, Sweet Basil: even you,
Lemon verbena: must exert yourselves now and
somewhat harden
Against untimely frost; I have hovered you and
covered you and kept going smudges,
Until I am close to worn-out. Now, you
Go about it. I have other things to do,
Writing poetry, for instance. And I, too,
Live in this garden.

EDNA ST. VINCENT MILLAY, "Steepletop"

Gardening Is Its Own Reward

What a joy life is when you have made a close working partnership with Nature.

❧ Luther Burbank

For love of gardening is a seed that once sown never dies, but always grows and grows to an enduring and ever-increasing source of happiness.

❧ Gertrude Jekyll

In joy or sadness, flowers are our constant friends.
We eat, drink, sing, dance, and flirt with them.

❧ Kokuzo Okakura, *The Book of Tea*

Yet no, not words, for they
But half can tell love's feeling;
Sweet flowers alone can say
What passion fears revealing.

THOMAS HOOD, *The Language of Flowers*

Flowers are made to seduce the senses:
fragrance, form, colour.

HILDA DOOLITTLE

There is no "The End" to be written, neither can you, like an architect, engrave in stone the day the garden was finished; a painter can frame his picture, a composer notate his coda, but a garden is always on the move.

MIRABEL OSLER